This Thing of Darkness

IPBOOKS.net
International Psychoanalytic Books

International Psychoanalytic Books (IPBooks)
New York • http://www.IPBooks.net

I0106096

This Thing of Darkness

Published by IPBooks, Queens, NY
Online at: www.IPBooks.net

Copyright © 2023 Lisa Dart

All rights reserved. This book may not be reproduced, transmitted, or stored,
in whole or in part by any means, including graphic, electronic, or mechanical
without the express permission of the author and/or publisher, except in the case
of brief quotations embodied in critical articles and reviews.

ISBN: 978-1-956864-62-5

This Thing of Darkness

'It is when you are asking about something that you realise you yourself has survived it, and so you must carry it, or fashion it into a thing that carries itself.'

Nox

Prologue

Certain they love each other, lovers doubt. (What if their beloved should stop loving them? Die?)

Doubt, according to Wittgenstein, only comes after belief. What stands fast, he thought, does so because of what lies around it.

In his final work, On Certainty, how, Wittgenstein asked, is it that we know our own name with unquestionable certainty? Or the trees we see, the towel we reach for? In short, how are we certain enough to doubt?

Any certainty we have has some connection with doubt and, therefore, with speculation, fact, proposition and all the other things that lie around it — language and silence, memory and forgetfulness, love and hate, sanity and madness, metaphor and metonymy, trees, light, mathematics, a hand, a towel, the colour red —

Blood.

And always, infinitely, in the warm breath of doubt, the cold certainty of death.

A.

"If you know

then why can't you say?"

If you do know here is one hand,

we'll grant you all the rest.

When one says that such and such a proposition can't be proved, of course that does not mean that it can't be derived from other propositions; any propositions can be derived from other ones. But they may be no more certain than it is itself.

proposition, n.

Something proposed for discussion or solution; a problem, a riddle; a parable.
Also in Logic.

Math. A formal statement of a truth to be demonstrated (cf. theorem) or an operation to be performed (cf. problem).

The action of setting forth or presenting something to view or perception.

Something which is asserted or avowed; a sentence or form of words in which this is done; a statement, an assertion.

A statement which is capable of truth or falsity; a mental formulation of that which is expressed by such a statement.

The action of proposing something to be done.

A matter, problem, or undertaking that presents itself for accomplishment, resolution, etc., esp. considered in respect of its likely ease or difficulty or prospects for success. Usu. with modifying word. Eg. A (tough, etc.) person to deal with.

114. If you are not certain of any fact, you cannot be certain of the meaning of your words either.

61. A meaning of a word is a kind of employment of it.
For it is what we learn when the word is incorporated into our language.

So, is that sprig of delicate white flowers with green memorial leaves on the kitchen counter a fact because in gardening journals and encyclopaedias this plant is called virburnum tinus and gardeners know it as such?

Or is it because lying around it are books, a glass and an old set of blue scales?

Or is it because virburnum tinus reminds me of a story I have always thought about writing? Something to do with a young child, a peasant hut and birds returning from their winter migration. The child, a girl, cares for a sick father. He lies on a simple bed. At the end of this imagined story, the girl will come rushing into him, pointing to the small skylight above his head to say:

'Look, father! Look! The brent geese are back!'

63. If we imagine the facts otherwise than as they are, certain language-games lose some of their importance, while others become important. And in this way there is an alteration - a gradual one - in the use of the vocabulary of a language.

Spring and hope are supposed to be conjured by the girl's words. And that is what they have to do with this unwritten story. With virburnum tinus, its winter flowering.

There are other unwritten stories that lie around virburnum tinus. I know there's another one because in this story virburnum tinus is given a private name. In this story the protagonist is L.

And I have wondered about L. for a long time. Her determination, her vulnerabilities, love affairs. As if it were possible, I have wanted to get back to the beginning. Her earliest memory. A beach. Her toes in damp sand and a lost sock (red?). That distant stretch of sea. The light.

L. doesn't know the proper name — the name agreed, Wittgenstein says, by a community bound together by science and education: virburnum tinus.

The private name is not bound like this; only L. and one other person know the private name. This name for virburnum tinus is the delicious one of intimacy.

When I think of the private name L. has for virburnum tinus something comes forth out of the cold, tells of new beginnings. Hope.

3 yrs?

Lots of love
Dad xxx

Fact:

1965

L. is four years old when her father tries to kill himself.

At fifty-one L. is standing in front of a black door with a knocker of a hand. Someone has suggested therapy — psychoanalysis.

L. doesn't use the knocker. She presses a very small, faded, red button on an intercom on the side brick wall and waits for a voice to say:

'Er, come in...'

' The Talking Cure '

"As a method of psychological help, psychoanalysis is based on the theory that early relationships with parents, childhood experiences of love, loss, sexuality and death all lay down patterns in the mind which provide unconscious 'templates', which have enduring effects on psychological functioning and are the source of conflicts which can block development."

THE INSTITUTE OF PSYCHOANALYSIS

The Talking Cure

Talking The Cure

the unsayable

The Talking

Sometimes L. doesn't know what to say to her therapist because sometimes words were inside her and sometimes they were outside her and sometimes they were the wrong words and sometimes there seemed to be no words...

Cure The Talking

Talking The Cure

The Cure Talking

psychosis, n.

Med. and Psychol. Originally: any kind of disordered mental state or mental illness.

Later: spec. severe mental illness, characterized by loss of contact with reality (in the form of delusions and hallucinations) and deterioration of intellectual and social functioning, occurring as a primary disorder or secondary to other diseases, drug ingestion, etc.; an instance of this.

Cf. neurosis.

275. If experience is the ground of our certainty, then naturally it is past experience.

L. is four years old. She likes parties. She is coming back from one holding a small pink telescope, smelling of newness. She put her hand into the gift box, felt its hardness. The door is open as other children are already leaving. A woman is smiling down at her. Not her mother. Dark outside, the hallway is lit. Warm and bright. The woman is smiling. A home.

L. is at her own house now. Little light. She moves cautiously from the hall to the back room. Her mother is somewhere. Is her mother talking to her? The new smell of the telescope is comforting. She clasps it tightly. The telescope is like Popeye's, but it belongs to her. Some things are far away. Some close-up, huge.

144.   The child learns to believe a host of things - i.e. it learns to act according to these beliefs. Bit by bit there forms a system of what is believed, and in that system some things stand unshakeably fast and some are more or less liable to shift. What stands fast does so, not because it is intrinsically obvious or convincing; it is held fast by what lies around it.

memory, n.

Senses relating to the action or process of commemorating, recollecting, or remembering.

An act of commemoration, esp. of the dead;

The action of remembering; recollection, remembrance.

To have memory (of): to recollect; also to have of (someone) in memory: out of memory: forgotten...

Now the party is L's. In her house. In the front room with bay windows. The carpet, black and white leopard spots. At the party L's friend gives her a present. She tears the blue paper off across a corner. There is a white paper edge under the blue.

A red book!

Out in the Sun.

A Ladybird book?　It is about Peter and Jane.

Jane has yellow hair. Her mother smiles. Jane helps mother in the kitchen. Jane smiles. They are making cakes.

'Aren't we having fun?' says Mother.
'Yes, we are having fun,' says Jane.

Peter has brown hair. His father has overalls on. Peter helps his father in the garage. They are mending the car.

'Aren't we having fun?' says Father.
'Yes, we are having fun,' says Peter.

'Fun,' says Peter.

'Fun,' says Jane.

L. throws the book across the room.

224. "I know that it never happened, for if it had happened I could not possibly have forgotten it."

But, supposing it did happen, then it just would have been the case that you had forgotten it. And how do you know you could not possibly have forgotten it?

I wonder what this book means for you? L's therapist says.

Jane likes to help Mummy. She wants to make cakes like Mummy.

"Let me help you, Mummy," she says. "Will you let me help, please? I can make cakes like you."

"Yes," says Mummy, "I will let you help me. You are a good girl."

"We will make some cakes for Peter and Daddy," says Jane, "They like the cakes we make."

new words

let will

This year
I chose
as subject
the psychoanalytic act.
It is
a strange
couple of words,
which, to tell
the truth...

Jacques Lacan

I am
proposing
Psychoanalysis.

It

IS

understood
as

at
least
in
principle....

....it is
supposed,
at
least
by
the
fact
that
you
are
here
to
listen
to
me,
that
psychoanalysis
does
something...

It
does.

That
is
not
enough.
This is
the
essential,
it
is
at
the
central
point.
It
is
properly
speaking
the
poetic
view
point
of
the
thing...

Jacques Lac

THE COODEN BEACH HOTEL

INVOICE

Wed 30-Mar-2011
VAT No. 850 9279 03
Page: 1

Room Account Statement

Room Bill For Room: 119 .

Number of Nights: 1

Trans Date	Description	Reference	Charges	Credits	Balance
29/03/2011	Toiletries	Brush & Paste	2.40		2.40
29/03/2011	Voucher Sales	BT 90mins	6.00		8.40
29/03/2011	Bar Drinks	EPOS POSTING	3.50		11.90
29/03/2011	Bar Drinks	EPOS POSTING	15.00		26.90
29/03/2011	Dinner	EPOS POSTING	42.90		69.80
29/03/2011	Tea/ Coffee	EPOS POSTING	2.00		71.80
29/03/2011	Standard Single Tari	[Accom Post]	60.00		131.80
	Total Charges:-		131.80		

I agree that my liability for this bill is not waived and agree to be personally liable in the event that the indicated person, company or association fails to pay for any part or the full amount of these charges. All accounts are due and payable on presentation.

SIGNATURE

Amount Payable   **£131.80**

HAVE YOU LEFT YOUR KEY?

The Cooden Beach Hotel Ltd
Cooden Sea Road, Bexhill-On-Sea, East Sussex TN39 4TT • Telephone 01424 842281 • Facsimile 01424 846142
Registered Office, 1 Reef House, Plantation Wharf London, SW11 3UF Company Number 05341915 vat no. 850 9279 03
www.thecoodenbeachhotel.co.uk

In L's intimate world viburnum tinus is known as 'snow blossom'.

verb: videre (to see)

I see.   I saw.

Did I see?

What did I see?

See-saw margery daw...

Musical chairs first, then another game. All the boys and girls are in a line. Everyone's arms are high above their head. Then there's singing:

'Oranges and lemons say the bells of St Clements...
And here comes a candle to light you...'

 L's mother went to bed by candlelight.
'I only used to have a candle.' Her mother says this quite often. (L. is scared of the dark.)

'A candle to light you...'

'Only a candle!' L's mother says.

L. knows this. A candle holder with a handle. She has seen it sitting sterile, wax-white near the white bowl with the huge jug in her grandfather's house, behind a curtain at the top of the stairs. It is clean, but L. imagines tear-like dripping on the side of the candle. She imagines climbing the narrow staircase with its deep stairs, the wallpaper browning, the damp patch, the picture on the stairs, the stairs hard to go up and the smell of the strangeness. The handrail is brown. Shiny, black metal holds it to the wall. L. is different here. Can she be someone new, holding a bright candle? She doesn't quite know who.

Not the girl ... Not the girl...Not the girl who...

388. …Is it more of a proof of the existence of external things, that I know this is a hand, than that I don't know whether that is gold or brass?

The room where she sleeps in her grandfather's house has holes in the corner. Spiders might come out. Spiders live in the toilet which is outside. The door is green with a clunking latch. The toilet paper is shiny like tracing paper. She smells the toilet's cold stinky smell. The rusted cistern is high up.

'Tell her not to pull that plug!' her grandfather says to her mother.

L. doesn't want to touch the handle, the rusty chain. She is quick to be out in the sun.

She doesn't know spiders come from anywhere.

A Monday, December 2011

L. is standing in front of a black door with a brass knocker of a hand.
There's a shrub (tree?) in the terraced garden. L. notices it now she has relaxed.
Pink buds, white flowers, perfectly formed snow blossom.

She doesn't use the knocker, but presses a very small, red button on an intercom
and waits for a voice to say…

L. wants to know the name, the 'proper' name. Later she googles trees and
shrubs, finds the name: virburnum tinus.

349. "I know that that's a tree" - this may mean all sorts of things: I look at a plant that I take for a ... and that someone else thinks is a... He says "that's a shrub"; I say it is a tree...Each time the 'that' which I declare to be a tree is of a different kind. But what when we express ourselves more precisely? For example: "I know that that thing there is a tree, I can see it quite clearly." –

Tree

In botany, a tree is a perennial plant with an elongated stem, or trunk, supporting leaves or branches.

Definition
Although "tree" is a term of common parlance, there is no universally recognised precise definition what a tree is, neither botanically nor in common language.

Trees are also typically defined by height, with smaller plants being classified as shrubs. However the minimum height which defines a tree varies widely, from 10 m to 0.5 m.

Trees differ from shrubs, which are also woody plants, by usually growing larger and having a single main stem; but the distinction between a small tree and a large shrub is not always clear, made more confusing by the fact that trees may be reduced in size under harsher environmental conditions.

Wikipedia

Ladybird

every age and every stage

A brief history of KEY WORDS

Written by British Educationalist William Murray and first published
by Ladybird in 1964. He wanted to know

which words a child needed to learn first...

The English Language has 400,000 words, 240,000 are main words, but
most people use 20,000 words. They discovered that of these 20,000 words,
relatively few made up a large percentage of all we use each day. If children
could learn these 'Key Words' first, William Murray knew...

Wikipedia

cAkeY

Off their Hinges

bonkeRs

BaⅰMy

swor(

sdwor

Unhinged

word

cra_cked

lunatic

wO-rds

off with the FAIRiES

three sheets in the wind

sdwor

dwosr

craZy

meNtal

queer in the head

one brick short of a FULL load

loony

psycho

nuts

Philosophy Forums » Metaphysics and Epistemology » Hinge Propositions and Their Epistemic Importance

Details Discussion (115) Print Report

Hinge Propositions and Their Epistemic Importance

•Sam26

Forum Veteran
Usergroup: Sponsors

#61 - Quote - Permalink
Posted 12/09/10 9:46PM:

A further point to make about the closure-principle may be this - generally we can use propositions to support other propositions, as in the case of the closure-principle. However, hinge propositions are the exception to the rule. That is to say, that although we can describe these kinds of beliefs using propositions, and we can plug them into logical rules of inference which yield a particular result - it may be the case, and I believe it is, that because of the nature of these beliefs we simply cannot treat them as other propositions.

Total Topics: 13

Total Posts: 872
♂

The flowers of virburnum tinus before they unfurl are pink, rounded, tiny buds. These flowers are common. In parks, hedgerows, gardens. In bloom, white. In mid-December, when the frost has come, dense and white.

And fleetingly, in my imagination, luminous.

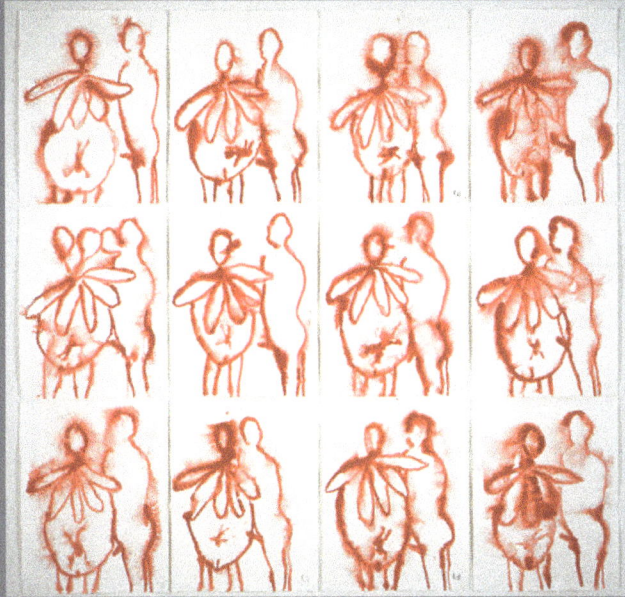

And he knew her…

Cf. Matthew 1.25

230. We are asking ourselves: what do we do with a statement "I know…"? For it is not a question of mental processes or mental states.

And that is how one must decide whether something is knowledge or not.

' The Talking Cure '

"Psychoanalysis is the name given to the theory of mind developed originally by Sigmund Freud, a theory which has had and continues to have an enormous impact on culture and intellectual life. Although there has been considerable development in the theory and practice of psychoanalysis since Freud's day, certain key ideas have retained their place and vitality within the theory.

These include:

- the discovery that there are large aspects of our psychological functioning which, though having a profound determining effect upon us, are largely hidden, that is, they are unconscious

- the recognition of the ubiquity of unconscious conflict

- the understanding that when human beings become involved in relationships with others, they bring to those relationships 'templates' derived from early childhood situations and transfer them into the current situation, that is they form transferences

- the recognition of the centrality of sexuality and aggression in mental life and that important aspects of this are laid down in childhood."

THE INSTITUTE OF PSYCHOANALYSIS

211. Now it gives our way of looking at things, and our researches, their form. Perhaps it was once disputed. But perhaps for unthinkable ages, it has belonged to the scaffolding of our thoughts. (Every human being has parents).

Nothing to remember!

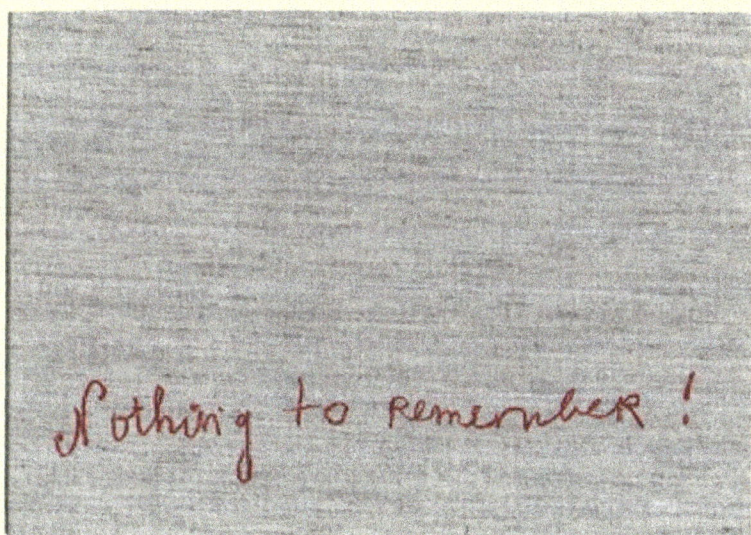

Snow blossom in your hand, then left on the kitchen counter…

…the ache I am reminded of…

And it was then, when she was fifty one, (March 2011), L. drove to the Cooden Beach Hotel.

Where, a month earlier, her brother had said matter of factly, as if it were a matter of fact/for fact, he wouldn't go to their funeral. Her parents'. And she had started to cry. Her nephew saw her tears. L. can still see the little boy's face. The lawn. The bridge. Dad-dy! he says.

In the hotel L. took a single room. Like a nun's cell. She phoned the man who loved her. She was not going home. He could come to eat with her in the hotel if he wanted, but she was not going back.

At supper, as they ate, the room seemed soft. There were candles.

And when she went back to her hotel room she looked at the small single bed. A spiritual vigilance she thought. And then she stared in the mirror at herself. And she thought she must cut her throat. And she extended her neck, pushing her head back in the mirror. She felt a thin sharp line drawn like a wire (perhaps?) across her throat. It hurt her. But the mirror held her. Her face. Her eyes. Her short brown hair. They seemed ugly. And then they seemed handsome. A gift. Not to be taken. And then inside her was that scream again, but she didn't scream.

The thin line across her strained neck hurt her. It was taut. Any more taut and it would cut her. Cut her. End her. And for a short time (how long?) this seemed right. What she should do. The right thing.

And then it wasn't. There in the mirror was her own face. And it held her. No. She shook her head. No. She would go to bed. Would she sleep? She didn't know. But she would go into her nun's bed. A single bed for the spirit. She would rest there. Not able to think anything. She would rest there. Not knowing.

352. If someone says, "I know that that's a tree" I may answer: "Yes, that is a sentence. An English sentence. And what is it supposed to be doing?" Suppose he replies: "I just wanted to remind myself that I know a thing like that"? –

Shrub

A shrub is distinguished from a tree by its multiple stems and shorter height, usually under 6 m tall. Plants of many species may grow either into shrubs or trees, depending on their growing conditions.

Wikipedia

In the morning she worried about the death of the human spirit. For the unappreciated, poor women who would clean her nun's cell. She would restore their dignity. She gave one of them forty pounds. And she sent her friend (the one who made a sculpture of her head) one hundred pounds. For the human spirit. To stop it dying.

And then later, in the hospital, (the first time) when they asked her,

'Did you feel like killing yourself?'

'Yes,' she said, smiling, 'but only for about three minutes'.

And she could smile. She knew that it was alright. She was proud of her honesty. Surprised by it. Yes, she had admitted it. It was a fact. But now she didn't want to die. She would not allow the thin-felt-sharpness across her neck to cut her.

But for quite a long time after, every so often, when she thought no-one would support her, no-one would help her when her parents died, if she stretched her neck up she would feel the taut line, the blade-like line across her throat, and she knew its steel, but though it hurt, it would not cut her.

She knew she would not let it draw blood.

340. We know, with the same certainty with which we believe any mathematical proposition, how the letters A and B are pronounced, what the colour of human blood is called, that other human beings have blood and call it "blood".

548. A child must learn the use of colour words before it can ask for the name of a colour.

The man in the sweet shop
likes Jane and Peter, and
they like the man.

He has the sweets they like.

We want the red ones,
please, they say

Get the red ones, please

new words

like   red

In the hospital (the first time) L. places a red scarf over the radiator by the window, over the gaping metal slits. Then she lays out all her things very carefully: books (Plath, Rilke,) tickets, credit cards, her red notebook. The one where she had written down ideas as fast as she possibly could, faster and faster, until the words disappeared and there were only marks on the page. Ones even she couldn't decipher.

And one morning in the hospital (she was there twelve days) out of the window she sees a red tulip and, for an instant, high in the sky on a bird's wing, blood. She knew with certainty the planet was dying.

After leaving hospital, L. takes the scarf to her therapist who spreads it out on the couch and stares at it, runs her hand over it, smoothing creases with her fingers carefully, lovingly, thoughtfully...

'Gosh, it's very red, with lots of eyes. Have you ever worn it? We will explore what it means for you, the significance of...'

L's therapist says,

'this colour red...'

Proposition:

Red is a redeemable referential.

At L's brother's party everyone is at a long table. Her mother's friend passes plates. The table is in the back room. Black French windows open onto a concrete patio. In the corner of the patio, on the flowers, butterflies tremble. A boy at the party called Christopher shouts across the table. His eyes are large, too large, behind his round pink glasses. The lenses are thick. The ends of the frames curve right round his ears with a steely springiness. He has freckles and he shouts across the table. L's mother slams down the plate she is holding. Her mother's friend's knuckles whiten around the jug she is carrying.

L. is frightened by the French windows, their metal frames, their blackness. And she is frightened by the carpet, which is red.

273. But when does one say of something that it is certain? For there can be dispute whether something is certain; I mean when something is certain, I mean, when something *is* *objectively* certain.

Fact:

Coming home early, the man who loves her puts on the stairs (so she will pick it up) some of the year's first snow blossom...

274. ...One such is that if someone's head is cut off he is dead and will never live again.

Experience can be said to teach us these propositions. However, it does not teach us them in isolation: rather, it teaches us a host of interdependent propositions. If they were isolated I might perhaps doubt them, for I have no experience relating to them.

275. If experience is the ground of our certainty, then naturally it is past experience.

Does L. say what Christopher says? Do the other children at the party say what Christopher says?

L's mother is very, very angry.

'If you ever say that again I'll wash your mouth out with soap and water! And don't think I don't mean it'.

L's mother says to her friend, 'You have to make children know.'

And L. knows her mother means it.

('Years later I dreamt of a massive spider rearing up over me.' L. says to her therapist.)

Perhaps the children at the party aren't just saying what Christopher says, perhaps they are chanting it. And then they are singing,

'Here comes a chopper...'

There's black paint on the windows, soap, bubbles, water...

L. is caught between two boys.

'Here comes a... to chop off your head...'

Blood?

A gAME of Languafe

"Sorn-off, sware-n off, sawn off

sore-off, eye-sore, arse-sore, sow-sore.

snore-saw, eye-saw, see, saw...

See-saw margary daw...

455. Every language game is based on words and 'objects' being recognised again. We learn with the same inexorability that this is a chair as that 2 x 2 = 4.

Objects:

Fluorescent strip light.　　　Ambulance.　　　Umbrella-stand.

As a method of reading, Ladybird books were known as the 'Look and Say.'

The fluorescent strip light is in the kitchen.

The ambulance has a flashing blue light.

The umbrella-stand is in a neighbour's house.

144. The child learns ....some things stand unshakeably fast and some are more or less liable to shift. What stands fast does so, not because it is intrinsically obvious or convincing; it is held fast by what lies around it.

ELEPHANT HUMIDOR
Uses for an Elephant's Foot

Elephants' feet were once used as cooking pots. Colonial Englishmen noticing how versatile they could be turning them into tobacco humidors, flower pots, calling cards and even umbrella-stands. The elephant's foot would serve as a unique conversation piece. Believe it or not!

Once, years ago, L. wrote a poem about all this – she shows it to her therapist.

Poem

Our Suburban Homes

Now over forty years ago, why does it matter?
I still remember odd things: the leaf-shaded porch
across the road; the strip-bright fluorescent
flick of light and an elephant's foot umbrella-stand,
huge, indelible grey with ridged yellow toenails.
Our neighbours back from India (he, an ex-colonel,
she, a nurse, down to earth) took us kids in.
I stared in blank shock at the umbrella-stand's height,
diameter, curve of nail, wrinkled skin: the grandness
of such an exotic thing in a semi on our tarmacked
Tubbenden Drive – umbrellas, walking sticks jutting out.
Today I imagine the elephant's lumbering bulk of fall,
wizened eyes petrified, dust, a thousand flies.
the red-raw hack of stumps and tusks -
and I recognise memory's concealing trick:
the kitchen light, blue flash of ambulance,
that umbrella-stand. Not the knife pressed
against your neck with consequential hand.

Hers is an inspirational story. But to focus on one person's experiences would be to ignore the testimonies of others who believe that their mental distress has biomedical roots. Indeed, many people report that they can see no clear reason for their distress and firmly believe their life stories have little bearing on their mental state.

Nevertheless the DCP believes the world of mental health treatment would benefit from a "paradigm shift" so that it focused less on the biological aspects of mental health and more on the personal and the social.

"In essence, instead of asking 'What is wrong with you?', we need to ask 'What has happened to you?'," Johnstone said. "Once we know that, we can draw on psychological evidence to show how life events and the sense that people make

'I remember having to take you and M. into a back room. I was that bit older, M. was that bit younger. You were in-between…a difficult age.' L's sister says.

One day because she wants the facts. To be certain of the facts. L. asks her mother what happened…

'We had gone out for the evening and your dad hit his head on the car as he was reversing. ('He fractured his skull basically,' L's sister says). He lost his memory. He couldn't remember how to get home. I had to drive. All the way home, he kept on saying,
'Promise you won't leave me. Promise you won't leave me.'
This liquid came out of his ear. It was on the pillow the next morning, and you know it's a funny thing to say, but your father never smelt the same again after that. Then, a few days later, on the Saturday morning, he went downstairs and...
I got a towel put it against his neck and phoned for an ambulance. Then I took the three of you over the road to Mr and Mrs Jolliffe. He was a colonel back from India. She was a nurse. It was very nice of them. They looked after you while I went to the hospital with your Dad. He was in hospital for twelve solid months. I used to go every day to see him and took the three of you at the week-ends. I always thought that was important.

And one day he discharged himself, came home took the car, the little money he had, his passport and ran off. You three children were all in school. I phoned the bank and they said all the money had gone from the account. I phoned the hospital too. They said there was nothing they could do. He drove to Dover… only came back because he didn't have enough money, I suppose, he wanted to go to Europe... But all that was a long time ago now.'

Happy Birthday to you

Happy Birthday to you

Hap -py

Years ago (I don't know when) L. dreamt:

A man is walking across a bridge. One hand on either side of his head. On his neck he is holding his sawn-off head. Between his head and his neck is a thin red line. As he walks his head keeps slipping.

'Interpretation... Interpretation... Interpretation...'

"The fact that dreams have at their command memories which are inaccessible in waking life is so remarkable and of such theoretical importance that I should like to draw still more attention to it...

One of the sources from which dreams derive material for reproduction – material which is in part neither remembered nor used in waking activities of waking thought – is childhood experience...

The third, most striking and least comprehensible characteristic of memory in dreams is shown in the choice of material reproduced. For what is found most worth remembering is not, as in waking life, only what is most important, but on the contrary what is most indifferent and insignificant as well."

Dreams... Dreams... Dreams...

544. Of course I may truthfully say "I know what this colour is called in English", at the same time as I point (for example) to the colour of fresh blood. But - - -

And then it was the time just before L. went to hospital (the first time) when the man who loved her was crying and crying, believing he was going to die. And then someone did die at the swimming pool. L. saw the body coming out on a stretcher, sack-clothed and eyeless.

And then another man, the one she worked with, (the one who wanted her, wanted her to find her voice, her own voice, write in her own voice, who wanted her to scream, a primeval scream), sat in her office at the school where she worked and when she didn't know what he wanted, he said to her: 'for fuck's sake talk to me!'

And then her brother said he wouldn't come to the funerals of her parents. So L. said her parents were dead. She told everyone this. Because she knew. And she locked herself in the bathroom. She began arranging everything in threes. The toothpaste, cleansers, shampoo bottles starting from the left. In blues and reds.

And L. and the other man (who had sat in her office one day, his head in his hands saying for fuck's sake talk to me!) would look after the man who loved her. They would carry him like Moses in a basket over the danger. She knew this. They would protect him. And then L. was singing and clapping:
'Swing low sweet chariot...coming for to carry me home.'
 And she knew the Munch picture on the bathroom wall, was her mother in spiritual preparation for death, looking 'over Jordan'. L. knew this. She saw it in the picture on the bathroom wall. She knew to open the window to let her mother's soul depart. And since her parents were dead, they wouldn't have to grow any slower, any older. L. knew this too. Like she knew their buckled backs, their buckled legs, their buckled faces, their buckled hearts. And her mother would push her father down the stairs, then kill herself. Her mother would cut her own throat with a razor blade. And dying together they wouldn't suffer. And then all the buckled-ness would be gone. L. knew.

And L. asked the man who loved her to come to her parents' house with her. She put a towel into a laundry basket. And the Paul Klee print of the pink house. She would cleanse her parents' house. Purify it. And she warned the man who loved her,

 'You will have to call the ambulance. There will be a lot of blood.'

It was Saturday afternoon and they were going out for tea at the Grand Hotel, 3.00pm. Then L. (who was sitting in the car with one hand on the steering wheel) urged her mother to cut her throat,

 'Go on, yes, you can do it.'

Then time itself split and disappeared. L. stared at the sun without blinking. She saw the black ring around it. And she screamed.

L. remembers nightmares, even right back then: blood on black faces, a man in black coming on all fours out of the wood, crawling in the yellow cornfield. In her house in Orpington she has a light bulb with butterflies inside. On all night, L. stares at the butterflies.

Her mother sings L's brother a lullaby,

'Go to sleep my darling...rest your pretty head.'

L. stares at the butterflies. Their wings, pointed and half-open. They are about to fly.

One night (and I know how much she loves him) L. wants her father to sing to her,

'Say you will, please, say...'

He can't. He doesn't know the words.

'Interpretation... Interpretation... Interpretation...'

"Another dream however, occurred to her – a dream she had first had when she was four years old and at the time the youngest of the family and which she had dreamt repeatedly since: A whole crowd of children – all her brothers, sisters, and cousins of both sexes – were romping in a field. Suddenly they all grew wings, flew away and disappeared.

It is not hard to recognise that it had been a dream of all her brothers and sisters. I may venture to suggest the following analysis. On the occasion of the death of one of these children, the dreamer not yet four years old at the time must have asked a wise grown–up person what became of children when they were dead. The reply must have been: 'They grow wings and turn into little angels.' In the dream that followed upon this information all the dreamer's brothers and sisters had wings like angels and – which is the main point – flew away. Our little baby-killer was left alone, strange to say: the only survivor of the whole crowd.

We can hardly be wrong in supposing that the fact of the children romping in a field before flying away points to butterflies. It is as though the child was led by the same chain of thought as peoples of antiquity to picture the soul as having a butterfly's wings."

Dreams... Dreams... Dreams...

'You were such a good girl!'

L's mother says.

The Talking Cure

'In three's, that's very Oedipal…perhaps, you know, your father's possible death has always been ahead of you?' ahead of you?'

Cure

L's therapist says.

The Talking

'A head?' 'Ahead?' L. knew this was insightful. In sight? 'A pun?' What exactly was 'in sight?'

Cure

Buckle, n.

A vigorous struggle or conflict.

Cure The Talking

L's therapist says.

Talking The Cure

The Cure Talking

'Staring at the sun…probably the very height of the psychosis.'

L's therapist says.

57. Now might not "I know, I am not just surmising, that there is my hand" be conceived as a proposition of grammar? Hence not temporally.

But in that case isn't it like this one: "I know I am not just surmising that I am seeing red"?

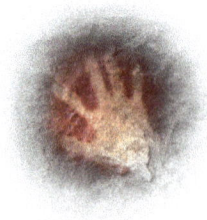

verb: Scirek (to know)

———————————

My father tried to kill himself...

I know (?) ...

▬▬▬▬▬▬▬▬

You know (?)

———————————

~~He knows~~

He knew (never said).

90. 'I know' has a primitive meaning similar to and related to "I see" ("wissen", "videre"). "I know" is supposed to express a relation, between me and a fact. So that the fact is taken into my consciousness.

(Here is the reason why one wants to say that nothing that goes on in the outer world is really known, but only what happens in the domain of what are called sense-data.)

This would give us a picture of knowing as the outer event through the visual rays which project it as it is into the eye and the consciousness. Only then the question at once arises whether one can be certain of this projection. And this picture does indeed show how our imagination presents knowledge, but not what lies at the bottom of this presentation.

A dream...

The aromatherapist suggests the treatment is to be cut down the spine, the shoulders opened.

The woman says to L. that it's ok her father has done it to her. She shows the scars across her shoulders. They are staggering. How could her father have done this to her?

She tells L. she will pour oils in. (L. thinks how much blood there must have been when her father did this to her.)

'Interpretation...   Interpretation...
Interpretation...'

"When the whole mass of these dream thoughts is brought under the pressure of the dream-work, and its elements are turned about, broken into fragments and jammed together – almost like pack-ice – the question arises of what happens to the logical connections which have hitherto formed its framework. ...the restoration of the connections which the dream-work has destroyed is a task which has to be performed by the interpretative process."

Dreams...   Dreams...   Dreams...

350. "I know that that's a tree" is something a philosopher might say to demonstrate to himself or to someone else that he knows something that is not a mathematical or logical truth.

Oedipal Complex

'Of all theories of relationships, Sigmund Freud's oedipal complex has probably caused the most controversy. It began with the study of a boy known as Little Hans. In 1909, Freud's paper, Analysis of a Phobia in a Five-Year-Old Boy, outlined Hans' fear of horses. Freud believed the boy's terror was due to feelings of anger he had internalised that related to his parents.

Freud theorised that all small boys select their mother as their primary object of desire. They subconsciously wish to usurp their fathers and become their mothers' lover. Typically, these desires emerge between the ages of three and five, when a boy is in what Freud defined as the "phallic" stage of development. Because the child suspects that acting on these feelings would lead to danger, desires are repressed, leading to anxiety.

The oedipal complex is named after Sophocles' protagonist, who unwittingly murders his father and marries his mother. There is a female equivalent, known as the Electra complex, but Freud was more concerned with what he termed female "penis envy".

Few people believe today that the oedipal complex has any real bearing on our lives.'

Sarah Wilson   **The Observer**, Sunday 8 March 2009

Electra Complex?

"I need you so that I could die
I love you so and that is why
Whenever I want you, all I have to do is
Dream, dream, dream, dream..."

The Everley Brothers

"Do Wah Diddy Diddy"

Manfred Mann 1965?

Do Wa Daddy...Did he?

Did he? Did he? Dum (b)... (what?) did he do?

B.

"was that a vision
                    or a waking dream?

fled is that music:-
                    do I wake or sleep?"

Around the name snow blossom lie subjective certainties of a shared world. I'm sure L. will never forget them: white sheets on the hotel's four poster bed, the small pub opposite a pink cottage on the road to Cley, the steaming bowls of the largest mussels, the long, low skies of Norfolk, where the sky seems hollowed out and the light, winter-bright, distant and where, if there were spirits, they would be...

Nor will she forget the brent geese with their faltering flight landing in a winter field. She has never seen or heard so many birds. The blunt clods of ploughed earth, in glancing sun, were shining.

'*Interpretation... Interpretation...*
Interpretation...'

"When we speak of the relation of dreams to mental disorders we may
have three things in mind: (1) aetiological and clinical connections,
as when a dream represents a psychotic state, or introduces it or
is leftover from it; (2) modifications to which dream-life is subject
in cases of mental disease; and (3) intrinsic connections between
dreams and psychoses, analogies pointing to their being essentially
akin.

Hohnbaum, quoted by Krauss, reports that a first outbreak of
delusional insanity often originates in an anxious or terrifying
dream, and that the dominant idea is connected with the dream...
The psychosis, says de Sanctis, may come to life at a single blow with
the appearance of the operative dream which brings the delusional
material to light; or it may develop slowly in a series of further dreams
which still have to overcome a certain amount of doubt."

Dreams... Dreams... Dreams...

dream, v.

To have visions and imaginary sense-impressions in sleep.

To behold or imagine in sleep or in a vision; sometimes with simple obj. = dream of.

To imagine or fancy as in a dream; to think or believe (a thing) to be possible; to picture to oneself.

To think of, even in a dream or in the remotest way; to have any conception of; to think of, or contemplate, as at all possible; to conceive, imagine. Chiefly in negative sentences (express or implied).

487. What is the proof that I know something? Most certainly not my saying I know it.

The second time

August 13th 12

In the park L. knew not to tell the man who loved her that it was worse still it was murder someone mother father had 'killed' someone had blood on their hands had plotted to kill her before she was born redness of interiority in her mind womblike vulnerable but she would forgive them her murderous parents for plotting against her and she would know their forgiveness or rather since that was the wrong way round they would know they were forgiven before they died...

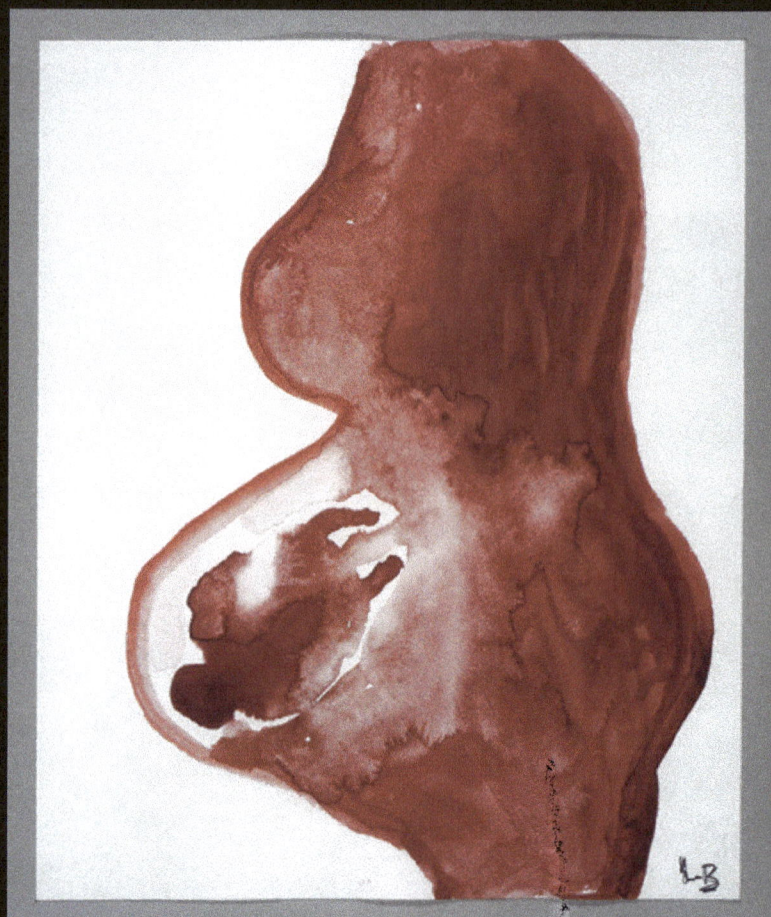

12. For "I know" seems to describe a state of affairs which guarantees what is known, guarantees it as a fact. One always forgets the expression "I thought I knew".

'they' were told by the doctor
to remove swords my father
had + I think he also had
          which he had on the
wall ?)

   I watched / I swa him
              ___
              ___
              🕷
        Eye spider (I spy
                    my little
                     eye!)

Slice huge bloody streaks
across the 'arse' (much too
beautiful to use that word) the
magnificent rounded haunches
of a black stallion. I (me)

L. wants to say to the white doctor in the hospital with the white coat and the white tablets ...

... the ambulance's blue light flashing, the fluorescent strip light in the kitchen and at our neighbour's house, in a corner in the hall, an elephant's foot umbrella stand, it had huge yellow ridged toenails...

In fact L. says:

I need more colour, more life, more spice, in my coloured life sliced by...
the knife **(?)**

My mother says her parents tried for six months before she was born to terminate her life. And they (my grandparents) got rid of the next baby after she was born... L. says to her therapist.

Anyhow, I don't trust Mum's account of things, she lives half in phantasy. L's sister says.

I almost forgot, but L. also says to the white doctor with the white tablets in the white coat, 'When I was four my father tried to kill himself and I …'

580. It might surely happen that whenever I said "I know" it turned out to be wrong...

the second time just before hospital (contin'd) (or as a diary...August 13th 12?)

... sitting on the bench in the park L. watched the small birds doves pigeons crows jauntily pecking at the ground and the roses how she stared at the roses and they were meant for her those pinky reds just to give their perfume their colours just for her how much richness in the world just for her how she knew it was just for her and she felt she might scream in the park sitting on the bench but then the red arrows came roaringly deafeningly overhead she couldn't see them but knew their red-pointed-redness all the same they bore her screaming yes the technological imperative of the world bore the screaming of all of them loud deep and thunderous they would scream for her for everyone and she could maintain her polite gentle well-mannered self she was a good girl and he (the other man the one who sat in her office and said for fuck's sake talk to me) was there rowing screaming out to God I want to die and the red arrows screamed out for him too vibrating the air so it shook - it shook in tremulous golds in the shimmer of delicacy that surrounded her in glory and screams screams of blood-red thunderous jets snorting and stampeding past her over her entering her heart paining her from inside and how green the grass was how green the trees with their silvers sunlit shaking the jets loud air-screams of accelerations exhalations over her head whoo whoo whoo...

Greece, Sept 12

Dear B

The other evening at a taverna, there was a small girl. A lovely child, about four years old who, on occasions, would dance to the Greek music playing. I could see how intense and uncomprehending she was. How captivating and bewildering the world... How she laughed when her mother played with her, (so affectionately). I began to understand much more fully, just how very small I was, when my father...

That's certain. But yet the pity of it...the pity...

Is the rage I expressed on the phone related to my feelings about my mother? Waiting long hours after school for her to come after work to collect me, because my father was in hospital? The school emptied of all the other children. Or going to someone else's house after school and waiting for her to pick me up. And waiting...

Perhaps your illness and the cancellation of the sessions mattered much more to me than I realized. Perhaps I felt let down and it activated 'uncontrollable rage'? (I had felt angry with you earlier on when you had said to me,'I don't do illness'. It seemed so lacking in humanity.) Feelings of loss, anger and despair may all have been re-activated by the sudden end to our sessions.

In my pocket there's a plush, though crumpled serviette from one of the tavernas. Which? I don't know. I only recall seeing white ones. You will guess what colour this one is...

L.

The weather is still cold, grey. Today L's therapist is wearing red. A long-sleeved, vibrant, red jumper with grey leggings and a grey over jumper with short sleeves. Such redness.

L. wonders about the choice of red.

Was it chosen purposely? An act of aggression, reconciliation or, an attempt to carry anger symbolically so to speak? Did you simply get dressed this morning without thinking that I might be coming and without all the possible signification of red that exists in me/between us? And does this matter? I suppose suddenly today it seems to and it has left me wondering. Today I've read two short pieces by Gertrude Stein. These too have left me wondering. A red stamp. A red hat.

'Your jumper looks nice' says L.

Which it does.

525.   What, then, does the case look like where someone really has got a different relationship to the names of colours, for example, from us? Where, that is, there persists a slight doubt or a possibility of doubt in their use.

18. "I know" often means: I have proper grounds for my statement. So if the other person is acquainted with the language-game, he would admit that I know. The other, if he is acquainted with the language-game, must be able to imagine how one may know something of the kind.

A Play

Act One Scene One (part of)

Dim spotlight on L. a young girl, aged about four, sitting crossed-legged on the otherwise empty blackened stage. Light gradually brightens, but not too bright, shadow of girl large (adult size)on the wall/floor and a butterfly above her head. Singing softly, hauntingly, her voice drawing out the words and humming parts something innocently eerie and rising in volume though never too loud as she repeats the song...

L: See-saw Margery Daw, Jack shall have a new master...penny a day...cos he can't work any faster...See-saw Margery Daw, what you did... arse sore...arse sore, Margery Daw, penny a day, what do you say? Can't you go any faster?

As spotlight lightens slowly audience can see L. has a daisy chain of buttercups and daisies. She is pulling off petals one by one as she sings. Appearing to have finished, where she was sitting strewn with petals, she gets up only to immediately get down on all fours, her bottom in the air. Grunts, makes animal noises, noses, sniffs the ground, grovels around on all fours:

L: Fucker, fucker, fuck! Must duck, pay the buck, face the muck, if you don't, won't truck...fucker, fucker fuck...see fuck, saw fuck, mustn't buck, need to tuck, cause a ruck, fucker, fucker, fuck...

As she reaches a good place (physically) to pause, light on her dims, she freezes on all fours, her bottom in the air, her face turned to audience. She's left frozen like this... frozen...

Light comes up elsewhere on stage. A pool of light. Audience realise they must have been there all the time,(i.e. not a change of scene.) Two women in a therapist's room. A is a woman in early fifties, sitting in a chair, opposite her therapist, B. another woman, older, but not easy to say her age...

A: ...and I tend not to finish things off, leave little bits over in pans, fridge, and so on... can't throw stuff away easily, though I have recently stopped doing this so much...

B: So what does this mean for you?

L. (high-pitched child tone in a clearly audible whisper, menacing, heard from the shadow): See-saw...can't ask for more... Margery Daw...arse sore...

A: (turns towards L. frozen, who stops singing and relaxes for a moment.)

L. (In sing-song nursery rhyme tone): needed time on the pot, to finish off, clot...didn't want to wipe my bot - anger was what I got...

A: (turns back to therapist): ...I think my mother invaded me, it made me angry, but I suppose I mustn't be? Perhaps as a child when I was naughty, being messy frightened her, not me..?

B: (smiling, looking at the clock): What we call in here... an infant's anal retentive power over a controlling mother...well, that's the theory...

A: Have I got any more time? Can I tell you one more thing?

B: (smiling holds up two fingers in a V-sign.) Two minutes...

A: My father's been on anti-psychotic drugs for fifty years...

B: How do you feel about that?

A: (about to cry rises from her chair leaves the therapy room).

L: (singing from the shadows): Pig, hog, buggery...goat and monkey...
yippee doodle dandy, dand-ee, dun-dee, dunce-see, dance-sea...

Catastrophic pitee!

Oedipal/Electra Complex?

Catastrophe

Violent crisis during which the subject, experiencing the amorous situation as a definitive impasse, a trap from which ~~he~~ she can never escape, sees ~~himself~~ herself doomed to total destruction.

A Lover's Discourse

R. Barthes

526.   If someone were to look at an English pillar-box and say "I am sure that it's red", we should have to suppose that he was colour-blind, or believe he had no mastery of English and knew the correct name for the colour in some other language. If neither were the case we should not quite understand him.

542.   "I can't describe this flower if I don't know that this colour is called 'red'."

'*Interpretation... Interpretation...*
Interpretation...'

"Any dream which one can remember clearly enough to describe it afterwards – any dream, that is to say, which is not a fever-dream – must always make sense, and it cannot possibly be otherwise. For things that were mutually contradictory could not group themselves into a single whole. The fact that time and space are often thrown into confusion does not affect the true content of the dream, since no doubt neither of them are of significance for its real essence..."

Dreams... *Dreams...* *Dreams...*

A hollowed out amputated foot of an elephant swirled as if on wheels centre stage. I noticed a coiled up hoover attachment, snake-like, corrugated inside it. Oh! I thought we're going there now, are we? (there was no blood 'their').

But then my father became an Indian warrior, prince-like, and took down   a sword from the wall of our house.

I watched/I _swa_/ him   eye spider   (I spy my little eye!)

slice huge bloody streaks across the 'arse' (much too beautiful to use that word) the magnificent haunches of a black stallion. I turned away. But I must have turned back again because he seemed to continue hacking until he had severed the horse's head completely from its body and the head was free floating in the air momentarily until it became a huge pantomime horse's head with thick red protruding lips (vivid like Mr Punch) large eyes and grotesquely laughing ...

Before hospital (the second time) the morning after her dream L. found herself inexorably drawn to the horse in the hall near to the umbrella-stand.

The horse was red and gold. I turned to look at its 'face'. Almost identical to the 'pantomime' horse in my dream: huge, red. The horse's rear was split open.   A wound.

Where she puts her hands.

On the wooden red and gold horse's wound.

Her hands – careful, tender, loving. She will heal the deep scar. The thin cloud scar she sees in the sky on bright blue days, the dark scar in the tarmac in the road to her therapist's that needs filling, the scar she imagines on the elephant; the scar, that thin white scar, on her father's neck.

She empties the umbrella-stand (how had I never noticed the elephant on it before, the indian prince?) and she washes it out, places it outside the door of their flat, she knows it will be cleansed out in the sun.

Later, she brings the umbrella-stand back in. And then she is singing: 'And He was high and lifted up and his train filled the temple, and his banner over me is love'; and she takes her time and already time is a vibrating purple light, (insight, in-sight?) inside her head and slowly, to atone for all the pain, to heal everything, she fills the umbrella-stand with flowers.

Long leafy stems with exuberant red heads.

I do ...   LB

The Talking Cure
Talking The Cure

'That dream seemed the most significant dream of my life...revelatory.'   L. says.

'Oh, they always do!   It was probably the onset of the second psychosis,'

L's therapist says.

'Yes, but I think my Dad really had a sword.'

'Perhaps you could ask your sister what she remembers...'

Cure The Talking

Talking The Cure

The Cure Talking

And in the summer at Holme-next-to-Sea the man that loves her is running. It is such a hot Norfolk sky day. He has a kite. It is very sunny and because (the fact of the matter) there is no wind he is running to keep the kite high in the sky.

And then there are those other times when L. thinks of the man who loves her as the stark figure he was one day, (black coat, black hat, black gloves) standing on the beach, no-one else around, at Wells-next-to-Sea before the horizon, low tide and, at the quay's end, the red lifeboat house. Far off, the black farewell signature of the geese.

And, now, she thinks only of his lips, snow-cold, warming hers, a winter blossoming…

Carluccio's Tunbridge Wells, ice cream melting in a glass dish in bright sun. The light-shades are red.

 What do you remember about Dad going into hospital?

L. says.

'The coal bunker, he…Mr Jolliffe… was a colonel or something. She was a nurse, I think. And they had - and I thought that it was wicked - this elephant foot umbrella-stand with huge toenails.'   L's sister says.

'Do you remember the ambulance at all?' L. says.

'No. I remember the sword.'

The see-saw is red.

The jumper is red.

The sweets are red.

The serviette is red.

The flower is red.

The plane is red.

The kite is red.

The towel is...

The crayon is...

The flags...

says Jane   says L's therapist   says L.

_____

new words

is   therapist   says

Right now L. wants to write about her father's gentleness. His hands.

How to convey the beauty of his hands?

~~His hands were beautiful.~~

~~His beautiful hands.~~

~~Beautiful, his hands.~~

~~Hands? His? Beautiful?~~

~~Hands, his – beautiful!~~

~~His hands...beautiful...~~

~~His hands on the hospital sheets even then~~
~~(when he was dying) were...~~

Hands...his?

solace: the stranger not found in regular doses... pills in paper cups colonise, each sad eye closes... L's hospital diary

676. "But even if in such cases I can't be mistaken, isn't it possible that I am drugged?" If I am and if the drug has taken away my consciousness, then I am not now really talking and thinking. I cannot seriously suppose that I am at this moment dreaming. Someone who, dreaming, says "I am dreaming", even if he speaks audibly in doing so, is no more right than if he said in his dream "it is raining", while it was, in fact, raining. Even if his dream were actually connected with the noise of the rain.

Fact:

The irredeemable regressiveness of red.

The Talking Cure

In the small room with pale green walls, a line of books, the green couch, the padded cushions how well her therapist listens. Accepts L's anger, her swearing, her stumbles, silences, her desire to know the facts, the fact of the matter in hand... a sword? Her desire to be sure, to know...

'But, remember, it is subjective certainties we deal with in here...'

says L's therapist.

And I know how grateful L. is to her therapist. (Though sometimes L. thinks she just doesn't get it and sometimes L. just doesn't get it.)

Grateful?

Her therapist is breath.

The Cure Talking

therapist, n.

Freudian 'unashamedly'; short hair, dark green dress
sometimes; a red jumper once, saying something about
'needing to cheer up the ghastly weather,' grey sleeveless
waistcoat, elephant grey; pearl earrings, patterned stockings,
black shoes with bows, spectacles (takes on and off),
looks at the clock, sassy, sharp, knowledgeable, baffled,
insightful, severe, kind, accepting, beautiful: like my mother
(transference?); not remotely like my mother (denial?); cites
Klein (envy) and Bion (who calls the psychiatric ward 'the brick
mother').

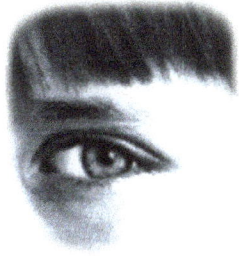

...spy with my little eye something beginning with...

S...

Mummy

Mum - me ?

Kent, Surrey and Sussex Partnership NHS Trusts
DISCHARGE NOTIFICATION AND PRESCRIPTION SHEET

To Doctor..._WILLIAMS_......   Practice _ARLINGTON ROAD_

PATIENT'S DETAILS:	
Name:	Date of Birth: 20.02.60
Address: _EASTBOURNE_	Consultant: _Dr. Lange_
	Ward: _BODIAM_
Hospital No:	Hospital: _DPP/ DGH_

Date of Admission: 30/3/11	Date of Discharge: 13/04/11
Reason for Admission: _Bizarre Behaviour_	Diagnosis: _Psychosis_.
Drugs COMMENCED during admission and reason: _Risperidone_	Drugs STOPPED during admission and reason:

Additional information for GP (e.g. blood test results, future monitoring requirements):

CRHT → follow up.

All drug allergies/sensitivities:

MEDICATION PRESCRIBED ON DISCHARGE   Pharmacist Screen (Signature & Date).............................
(State all drugs, not just those requiring dispensing)

Drug (Approved Name)	Dose	Frequency	Route	No. of Days	GP to continue Y/N?	Additional Instructions for G.P.	Pharmacy to supply Y/N?	Pharmacy use only
Risperidone	2mg	ON	O	14				

Prescriber name & designation (in capitals)....._VENKAT G ST1_........ Date..._13/4/2011_

Prescriber signature....._GK_........   Contact No............

For follow-up arrangements see Care Programme Approach (CPA) form

Care Co-ordinator............   Contact No............

The man who loved her brought her clothes to the hospital in a blue sport's bag.

Tucked in the side pocket – a small sprig of snow blossom still wet with mo(u)rning rain.

Freud: Infantile Sexuality and Oedipus/(Electra) Complex

- Erotic attachment of a child for the parent of the opposite sex
- Hostile or jealous feelings toward the parent of the same sex
- This might be a source of adult personality disorder when unresolved
- Psychoanalysis uncovering repression of the suppressed conflict in order to avoid the resulting anxiety

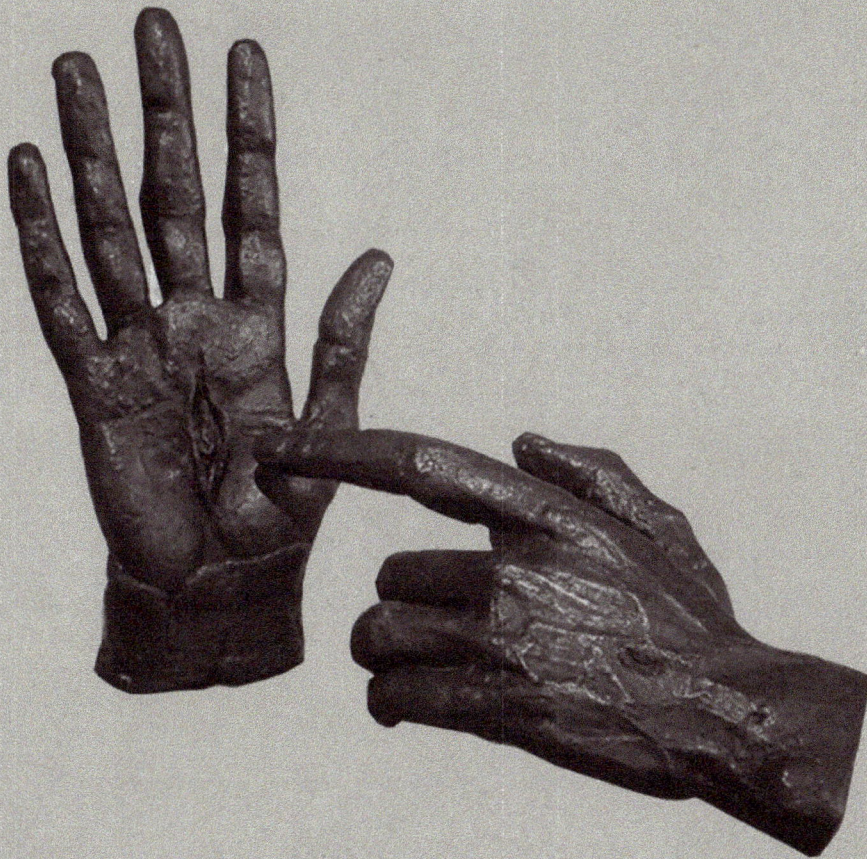

- **Erotic attachment of the child for the parent of the opposite sex**

- **Hostile or jealous feelings toward the parent of the same sex**

- **This might be a source of adult personality disorder when unresolved**

- **Psychoanalysis –uncovering repression of the suppressed conflict in order to avoid the resulting anxiety**

...BERWELL HOSPITALS MANAGEMENT COMMITTEE

ST. FRANCIS' HOSPI...
CONSTANCE ROAD
S.E.22

15th April, 19 65

Telephone :
BRIXTON 9941

Ref _____ JAB/AP/A.17049

Dr.Scott,
1 Knoll Rise,
ORPINGTON, Kent.

Dear Dr.Scott,

re:-Mr. .... - age 39
8 Tubbenham Drive, ORPINGTON, Kent.

This is just to inform you that your patient was discharged from here on the 13th April 1965 with a diagnosis of probable schizophrenia.

As you know he had become jaundiced after receiving Chlorpromazine and recent function tests have been returning rapidly to normal, Serum bilirubin being 1.8% on the 9th April,1965.

He was discharged on tabs Stelazine 10mgm.b.d and Amytal at nigh Perhaps you would be kind enough to supply these tablets as necessar and an appointment has been made for him to see Dr.Russell at the Maudsley Hospital in due course.

Yours sincerely,

J.A.BONN.

563. One says "I know that he is in pain" although one can produce no convincing grounds for this. – Is this the same as "I am sure that he..."?–

No. "I am sure" tells you my subjective certainty.

Chairman :
Viscount SANDON, T.D.

se Governor and Secretary:
L. H. W. PAINE, M.A.

Patron :
H.R.H. PRINCESS MARINA, DUCHESS OF KENT

THE MAUDSLEY H
DENMA

JLTB/MC/T.0331.

Dr. A. Scott,
296 Tubbenden Lane,
Farnborough,
Orpington, Kent.

Dear Dr. Scott,
     re: ██████ age 42,
       8 Tubbenham Drive, Orpington, Kent.

dose of Trifluoperazine 2 mgs. t.d.s. and Orphenadrine Hydrochloride
50 mgs. t.d.s.

spent at home. While in hospital there was a very slow improvement
Phenothiazines, but because of Parkinsonian side effects he at first

He has had skull X-rays which were as before, normal, and is having
an electrocardiogram tomorrow. I will see him again on Monday. I
have frequently discussed his case with Dr. Russell but it is very
difficult to know what one can do. I recently prescribed Imipramine
and increased the dose to 75 mgm. with some alleviation of his
subjective depression. On Monday I added Diazepam 10 mgm. t.d.s.

refused to take his tablets and a trial of a depot injection of Flu-
phenazine was made, but this produced severe extra pyramidal symptoms.

As you may know, he is thinking of returning to Plymouth where
wife's family live and where he thinks things will be rather easier
him. He seems to be holding down his present job quite well and has,
fact, recently been promoted. I think much the most important thing
that he should stay on Stelazine indefinitely.

     Yours sincerely,

15. It needs to be shewn that no mistake was possible. Giving the assurance 'I know' doesn't suffice. For it is after all only an assurance that I can't be making a mistake and it needs to be objectively established that I am not making a mistake about that.

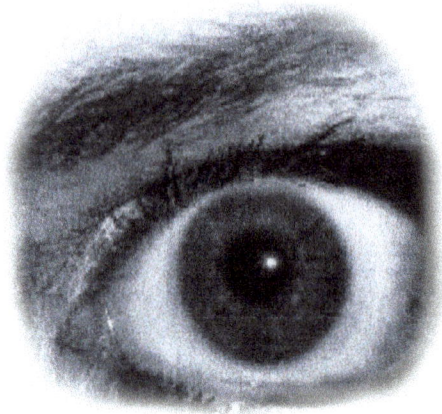

'I see/saw with my little eye...'

in the . . .

KiTcheN?

F A the R

MY

KiTCHeN?

H All?

tRylnG to ...

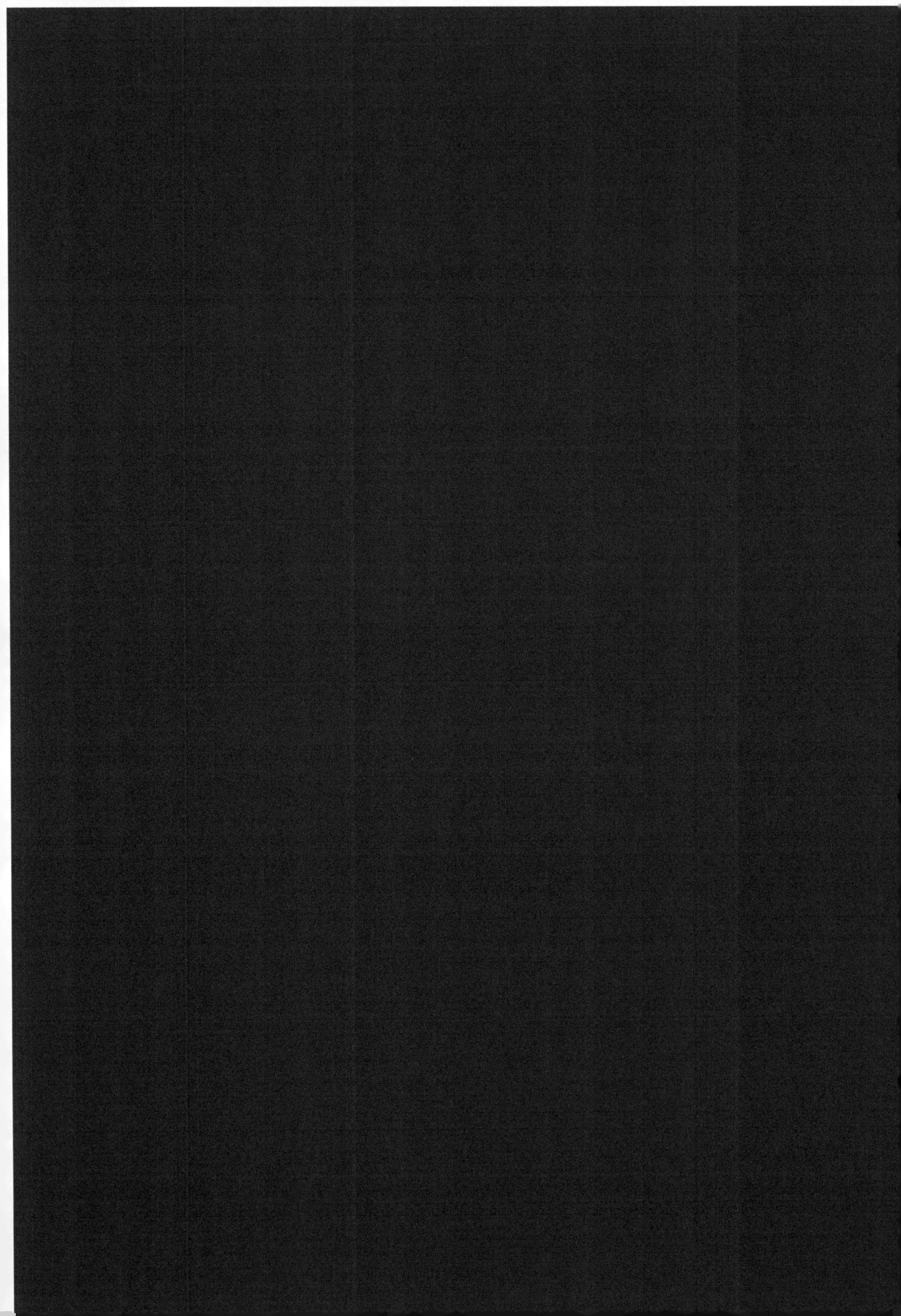

3. "So much to say...

say what you mean,

mean what you say!"

September 10th 12

'I am sanguine that it didn't last long. I get the feeling you enjoyed yourself — all that punning with the doctors.'

                                        L's therapist says.

'Yes', L. says.

(Was that true?) She thinks of how it was the middle of the night, how the curtain wouldn't close, how it hung half off its track, and how the lino was blunt to her eye, cold to her feet, and how cold the metal frames of her window. And how the blacked-out windows opposite stared in. How she heard screams. How she knew a child was dying, how her breath came in huge gasps, whoo, whoo…

And how afraid she was.

L. kept the word "sanguine". I found it surfacing in her mind at odd moments; she wondered about its "meaning":

sanguine, n. & adj.

blood-red, of, or pertaining to blood; consisting of or containing blood. Now rare. Of persons and expectations: with reference to some particular issue, hopeful.

'That word', L. says to her therapist later, when she checked its meaning.

'Something between us… the play of red and blood.'

162. In general I take as true what is found in textbooks...for example. Why? I say: all these facts have been confirmed a hundred times over. But how do I know that?

Lacan's interpretation of psychosis

"Lacan sought to address… the difference between psychosis and neurosis, as manifested in and indicated by language usage.

It was common analytic ground that 'when psychotics speak they always have some meanings that are too fixed, and some that are far too loose..."

(Sometimes L. thought words were inside her and sometimes they were outside her.)

"…they have a different relation to language, and a different way of speaking from neurotics'. Freud, following Bleuler and Jung, had pointed to 'a number of changes in speech...words are subjected to the same process as that which makes the dream".

66.   I make assertions about reality, assertions which have different degrees of assurance. How does the degree of assertion come out? What consequences does it have?

We may be dealing, for example, with the certainty of memory, or again perception...

Proposition:

My father tried to kill himself and I think I saw it.

Fact:

For nearly fifty years L. can't say, can't say, can't really say this to anyone.

Not even to herself.

"Whereas a metaphoric interpretation would consist in supplying another signifier which the signifier in the text stands for (a means b; the tie represents a phallus) a metonymic interpretation supplies a whole context of associations. Perhaps this metonymic interpretation might be called feminine reading...

Feminine metonymy has tricks and detours that according to Lacan, allow it to "get around the obstacles of social censorship".

Lacan's statements on language need to be taken in two directions – towards the fixing of meaning itself (that which is enjoined on the subject), and away from that very fixing to the point of its constant slippage, the risk or vanishing point that it always contains (the unconscious).

...the two vectors of language are "that which is enjoined on the subject", that is the law, the rules of grammar or propriety or identity, and "the unconscious" that which speaks in parapraxes"

Fact:

On the hotel door, (The Crown, Norfolk), a black coat, a black hat and on L's pillow - green leaves, pink buds, white flowers, as if words...

393. The sentence 'I know that that's a tree' if it were said outside its language game. Might also be a quotation (from an English grammar-book perhaps). But suppose I mean it while I am saying it?' The old misunderstanding about the concept 'mean'.

But there was the time (August) the day after they came back from the park when he saw her in her dressing gown; when he saw her unseeing eyes; when he saw her grab the red bathroom towel; when he heard her shouting 'this much blood!'; when he saw her slashing her finger across her throat again and again; when he saw her down on all fours; when he saw her run her fingers down her face as if she was crying; when he knew she didn't know what she was doing and he was so alarmed the man who loved her phoned her therapist who wanted to speak to her.

L. screamed down the phone:

Motherfucker!!

Mother, fucker?!?

Mother! (you) fucker !!! (?)

L. banged her fists on the paintings. She lay on the floor. She leaned her shoulder and bowed head against the wall. She wouldn't go with the ambulance men when they came. She didn't know, and they didn't know her anger, her sadness. She shook her head at them and pressed it against the wall in anger. Sadness.

510. If I say "Of course I know that that's a towel"... I have no thought of a verification... I don't think of past or future...It is just like directly taking hold of something, as I take hold of my towel without having doubts.

Interpretation... Interpretation...

"An acute observation by Greisinger (1861, 106) ideas in dreams and psychoses have in common the characteristic of being fulfilments of wishes. My own researches have taught me that in this fact lies the key to a psychological theory of both dreams and psychoses.'…the rapid sequence of ideas in dreams is paralleled by the flight of ideas in psychoses. In both there is a complete lack of a sense of time…

It is also worth mentioning those cases in which a word appears in a dream which is not in itself meaningless but which has lost its proper meaning and combines a number of other meanings to which it is related in just the same way as a 'meaningless word' would be…"

Dreams... Dreams... Dreams...

"I Want To Hold Your Hand"

The Beatles 1963
            (and everafter)

" Oh please, Daddy, ...
I wanna be your girl...
I wanna hold your hand... "

Proposition, n

A proposal or invitation to engage in sexual activity, esp. of a casual or illicit nature; a sexual advance or 'pass'.

Freud: Infantile Sexuality and Oedipus/(Electra) Complex

Illicit, adj.

Not authorized or allowed; improper, irregular; *esp.* not sanctioned by law, rule, or custom; unlawful, forbidden.

 illicit process n. *Logic* a form of syllogistic fallacy in which a term not distributed in the premises is distributed in the conclusion.

1691   H. Aldrich *Artis Logicæ* i. iii. 18   Quælibet Figura excludit adhuc sex modos. Nempe 1. Propter Medium non distributum... 2. Propter processum majoris illicitum... 3. Propter processum minoris illicitum.]

1827   R. Whately *Elem. Logic* 88   To infer a universal conclusion [from a particular minor premise] would be an illicit process of the minor.

1900   *Philos. Rev.* 9 386   The fallacies of illicit process and of undistributed middle.

1942   *Mind* 51 98   Fallacious conversion... In the categorical syllogism it appears as the undistributed middle or as the illicit process.

1979   *Ethics* 89 410   Is there not somehow an illicit process here from fact to right, or from 'is' to 'ought'?

October 12th 12

Dear B,

A very vivid dream last night...the central part...I was on some rocky ground that was in some way sacred and a sense of trying to do magic tricks among us. (A crowd?). I had my partner's hat and there was a faint red smudge on the top of one side. I began to feel some movement under the hat and then saw a slight moving bulge on the top and felt distinct movement around my neck.

Two birds, doves, emerged - one from the top of the hat; the other I took from my neck, felt its quiet, gentle, pulsing, feathered roundness as I held, then released it into the air with my hand.

Then from somewhere, possibly from the hat, I had a small red book which opened like a concertina and which I knew to contain secret sacred texts. Somewhere in the book or somehow I had a cheque. In the box where you would normally write the numbers for the amount to be paid was written: 'THE WORD'.

How to read this?

L.

September 15th 12

My sister over from Australia. Carluccio's in Tunbridge Wells, red light-shades, teacups, saucers, ice-cream in the glass dish melting in the sun.

'Are you sure it was a sword?' L. says.

'It was definitely a sword he was waving it about... I'm not a fool, you know, I know what he did. Why do you want to know?'

L's sister says.

See-Saw

I Spy

sdwor

aRsE Saw

I saw...

WORDS

SROWD

See.

EyE sOrE

I saw.

Daw

ARSE soRe

Saw.

WORDS

sdwor

MaRGeRy dore

I SWORE

Say it with flowers...

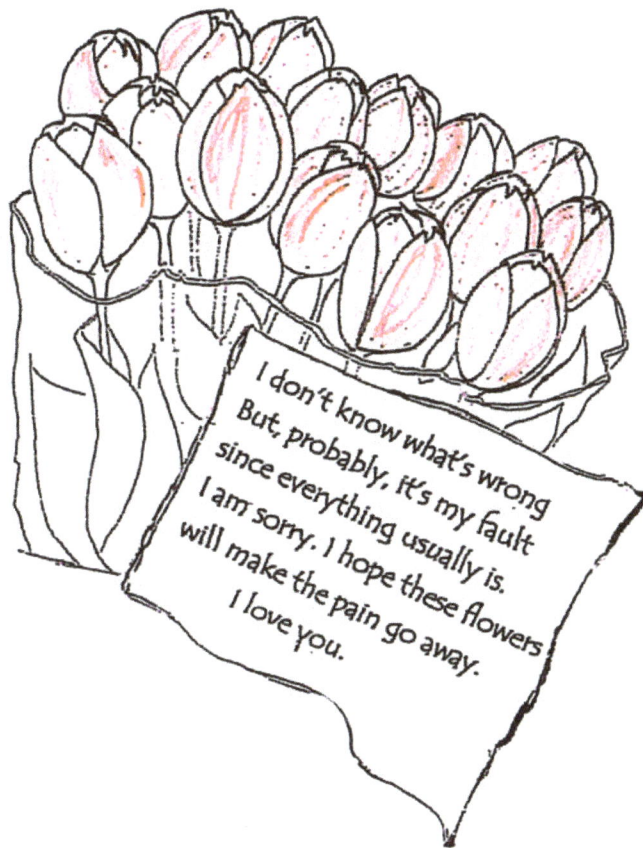

I don't know what's wrong
But, probably, it's my fault
since everything usually is.
I am sorry. I hope these flowers
will make the pain go away.
I love you.

Happy Birthday to you...

Proposition:

I think I saw a lot of blood.   L. says.

Fact:

Oh, you would have, L's sister says.

10. I know that a sick man is lying here? Nonsense! I am sitting at his bedside. I am looking attentively into his face.

_ So, I don't know, then, that there is a sick man lying here?

Neither the question nor the assertion makes any sense...

And "I know that there is a sick man lying here" used in an unsuitable situation, seems not to be nonsense but rather seems matter of course, only because one can fairly easily imagine a situation to fit it, and one thinks that the words 'I know that' are always in place where there is no doubt, and hence even where the expression of doubt would be unintelligible.

'I used to take you all to the Maudsley to see him every Sunday,' L's mother says. 'You remember the wall in the hall at Tubbenden? He was that yellow...'

And L. does remember how yellow her father's face looked.

And she remembers the sun on the hospital lawn. She remembers running up a bank. She remembers the frill on her dress. The large red cherries on the frill of her dress are close-up. The other people there are far away from her. Staring at her from their distance. A long way off. Not seeing. Not knowing.

And she remembers her father sitting (on a bench?on the bed?) with his hands clenched and his legs crossed tight, not saying anything in the glance of the sun.

And then she is at home in Orpington. It is summer. And it is still light. On her way up to bed she sits on the stairs at the bend by the window. She sits in the light. Now she is five years old. She stares at the carpet, the red stair rods in the sun's glance.

The hospital, yellow, red, and the scream inside, her father not being there.

Find Colouring Page: Blood Search

Search by Alphabetical Order

ABCDEFGHIJKLMNOPQRSTUVWXYZ

Online Colouring > Search Results

No colouring page found

Previous   Next

Proposition:

My father tried to cut his own throat with a sword.

Fact:

I know. I saw it.

28th November 12

Dear B,

On Monday evening I had a terrifying nightmare: I was in my parents'
bedroom possibly, but it also felt like a hotel room and a room in my brother's
apartment in America. The walls were a dark green colour; my mother was
somewhere in the background. Dark, black marks (rounded) appeared on the
walls...

On one wall they became red and two eyes and a sword shape appeared. I knew
that there was blood on the other walls. The black marks were blood. I knew
this. My brother ran into the room and fell to the floor. He lay there (sort of)
on his knees with his head in his hands, his bottom slightly in the air. His
hair was very black and thick. He was sobbing out 'I'm sorry, I'm sorry I lost
it'. I may have put my hand on his hair. Somewhere out in the passage way
(hall?) his small son was running saying/shouting 'Daddy!'

This woke me terrified. I lay in the semi-dark of the bedroom watching car
headlights flash/slash light scarrings through the Venetian blinds, trying to
calm myself, thinking I would call you in the morning for an extra session.
I was so frightened - the last dream I had like this, so vivid, you saw as the
onset of the psychosis...

L.

15. It needs to be shewn that no mistake was possible. Giving the assurance 'I know' doesn't suffice. For it is after all only an assurance that I can't be making a mistake and it needs to be objectively established that I am not making a mistake about that.

The Talking Cure

Talking The Cure

'Objective truth can't hurt...objective truth doesn't kill you, you know. There are important things to remember here: stay with the facts. Neurotics push them away into the repressed symptom. On the other hand, and this is very important for psychotics where there is a denial of reality, the facts...'

L's therapist says.

Cure The Talking

Talking The Cure

The Cure Talking

145. One wants to say "all my experiences shew that it is so". But how do they do that? For that proposition to which they point itself belongs to a particular interpretation of them.

"that I regard this proposition as certainly true also characterises my interpretation of experience."

viburnum tinus

From Wikipedia, the free encyclopedia

Viburnum tinus is a species of flowering plant in the family Adoxaceae, native to the Mediterranean area of Europe and North Africa. Laurus signifies the leaves similarities to bay laurel.

Scientific name: Viburnum tinus

Rank: Species
Higher classification: Viburnum

It is a shrub (rarely a small tree) reaching 2–7 m (7–23 ft) tall and 3 m (10 ft) broad, with a dense, rounded crown. The leaves are evergreen, persisting 2-3 years, ovate to elliptic, borne in opposite pairs, 4 -10 cm long and 2- 4 cm broad, with an entire margin. Pollination is by insects. The flowers are fragrant. The flowering period is from October to June. The flowers are small, white or light pink, produced from reddish-pink buds in dense cymes 5-10 cm diameter in the winter.

272. I know = I am familiar with it as a certainty.

174. I act with complete certainty. But this certainty is my own.

177. What I know, I believe.

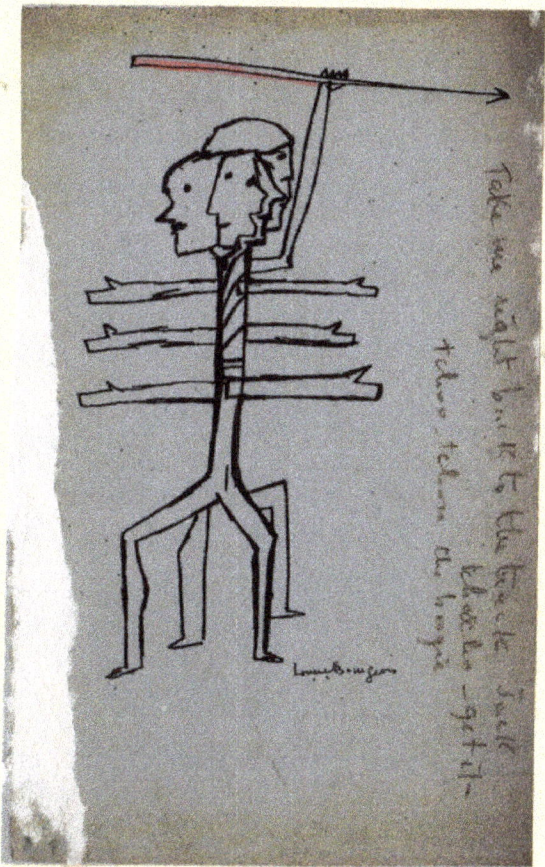

Take me right back to the track Jack
th..... th.... get it—
th..... th... at back

Louise Bourgeois

Sword

Username: ⌐   Password: ⌐

Register / Forgot Password

Hinge Propositions and Their Epistemic Importance

•Sam26   #61 - Quote - Permalink
                        Posted 12/09/10   9:46PM:

Forum Veteran
Usergroup: Sponsors

Those of you that are familiar with *On Certainty* know that Wittgenstein was responding to Moore's claims to know.

Wittgenstein responded to Moore's arguments by saying that the kinds of propositions that Moore thinks he knows, are not the kinds of propositions that one can neither know nor doubt.

They are propositions (**hinge propositions**) that fall outside our epistemic system. They are propositions that generally can neither be known nor doubted.

Some examples of hinge propositions are:

I live on the earth.

I have two hands.

2+2=4

I am a person.

Total Topics: 14

Total Posts: 878
♂

I am a person.   (He is a person.) I am

a person...he was ... I am... I am...

343. But isn't it that the situation is like this: We just can't investigate everything, and for that reason we are forced to rest content with assumption. If I want the door to turn, the hinges must stay put.

The Talking Cure

In the pale green room with its case of books, green couch, coloured tapestry cushions, brown leather chair, small clock and the one pot plant L. says to her therapist:

'They were Ladybird books – red covers. (L. is smiling.) I couldn't say fuck Peter and Jane then. Was I jealous of them having fun out in the sun? I couldn't say...couldn't say (what?) the chasm, a chasm, that chasm... all their certain fun...going on happily ever after... and *says* not *said*...? Always present, between life and death... all that infernal (eternal?) saying...'

341. That is to say, the questions that we raise and our doubts depend on the fact that some propositions are exempt from doubt, are as it were like hinges on which those turn.

L's father wore two watches in hospital. Whenever he moved his arms, time slipped round his bone wrists evasively. She hasn't forgotten the oxygen mask, his frail chest heaving, his head jerking and jerking, his mouth open. And the various drips, the fans, the groans and the rambling calls: for scissors to cut off all his bandages (the man opposite), for help to go to the toilet (the man on the left with a huge Band-aid pad on his head), and the sign in the entrance to the ward:

The month is June.

The day is Tuesday.

The season is Summer.

The weather is warm.

The next meal is supper.

The outlook is:

SUN

She remembers that last Sunday afternoon. So quiet, it was as if one of the doves flitting around outside had landed on the roof above their heads. And she saw death rising in his grey eyes. (Remember - that word with its... what did Barthes call it ...vibratory, or valedictory, halo?). And now in my mind's eye I see L. in a brightly lit room writing...

the sky is imperceptibly lighter and, far away, like an indecipherable sentence, the brent geese are coming more and more clearly into focus. Seeing this, the small girl calls out to her ill father.

'Look, father, the brent geese are back! Look!'

The Talking Cure

1.15pm. Cold, grey and raining. I am standing in front of a black door. The virburnum tinus leaves in the small patio garden are wet. (L. wants to let her therapist know she is breath, warm breath, but she doesn't know how.)

She presses the very small red button on an intercom and waits for a voice to say, 'Er, come in...'

Before the invitation always the small hesitation.

I wonder about that small hesitation - does it suggest doubt ?

Can one say: "Where there is no doubt there is no knowledge either?"

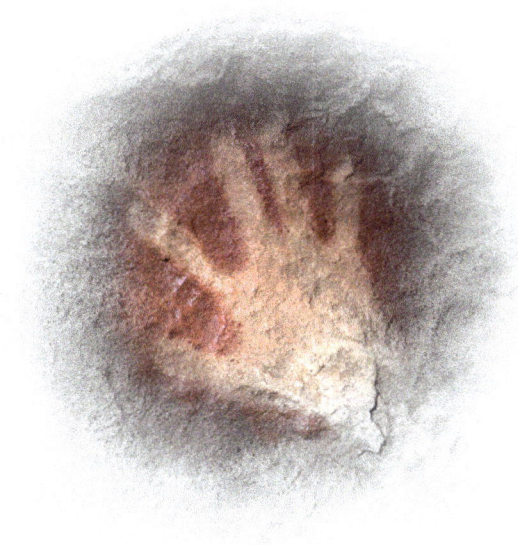

Epilogue

facts   facts   facts   facts   facts   facts

L. did talk to the man who sat in her office with his head in his hands saying 'for fuck's sake…' for five hours in the hospital (the first time) when he visited her.

L's sister went back to Australia at the end of her very short stay in England. September 12. They sometimes talk on the phone.

L. visited her father every day for the ten days before he died. He died June 11th 2013. 4.20pm. Before L. went in to see him at about 5.00pm, the nurse said, and was she crying, 'I'm so sorry, we couldn't close his mouth'. L. saw his wax-white face and his mouth still open as if, perhaps, he had something to say…

L's mother (alone, her face so sad) said to L.

'You know I never thought it would be like this. I imagined he would have a fall. And I would finish myself off. We had been happy until that week, that morning in the hall…it was horrific…I heard him go downstairs. I went to the top of the stairs and saw him and thought, Christ, what have we got here…He was homeless, you know, even when I first met him he was sleeping in the YMCA… Even after everything, I never told him to go, never once, I never said he didn't have a home here. It was only his own violation. I always thought your father was a good man.'

Her mother is crying when, moving hers like he did, she says, 'I miss his hands.'

L's brother did come to the funeral, he said a few words.

After the funeral L. went to the Normanhurst care home on the seafront at Bexhill, to pick up her father's things. The sun and blue sky complete; the sea — white in the wind, the gulls and yachts carried far out. On the beach wild, tormented, restrained by masts, the red flags…

L.'s therapist continues to work hard with her. Sometimes L. finds this very hard. 'Well,' her therapist says, 'how long do you want to be in therapy? Twenty years?' L. doesn't remember when, quite recently, her therapist mentioned *The Scarlet Letter*.

Ludwig Wittgenstein died on the 29 April 1951.

And only the other day (August 26 2013) the man who still said he loved her, gave L. an immaculate sprig of snow blossom. She put it for a moment on the kitchen counter between some books, a glass and the old blue scales.

immaculate, n: cf. spotless, stainless, faultless. Hopeful?

AcKnowledgements

(**facts** to be **grateful** for.)

This thing of darkness (I acknowledge mine), 'The Tempest', Shakespeare.

It is when you are asking... 'Nox, Anne Carson.

All the numbered quotations are, as implied, from Wittgenstein's 'On Certainty'.

Popeye seems to speak for himself, but is a creation of the American cartoonist E.C. Segar.

And he knew her (not), Matthew 1.25. Authorised King James Bible.

Images of Peter and Jane are published by the British publishers, Ladybird Books. The books make use of the whole word or "look and say" technique which is generally considered outmoded as a method for learning to read.

Ladybird images are as follows:

'5b Out In The Sun' by William Murray, illustrated by Frank Hampson (cover image, ref. kw_014)
© Ladybird Books Ltd, 1965
Reproduced by permission of Ladybird Books Ltd.
- '1b Look at This' by William Murray, illustrated by Martin Aitchison (butterfly image, ref. kw_002_01_003)
© Ladybird Books Ltd, 1964
Reproduced by permission of Ladybird Books Ltd.
- '3a Things We Do' by William Murray, illustrated by Harry Wingfield (cooking with mother image, ref. kw_010_01_002)
© Ladybird Books Ltd, 1964
Reproduced by permission of Ladybird Books Ltd.
- '3a Things We Like' by William Murray, illustrated by Martin Aitchison (sweetshop image, ref. KW_007_02_018)
© Ladybird Books Ltd, 1964
Reproduced by permission of Ladybird Books Ltd. Territory: UK.

Pages with Interpretation and Dreams come from 'The Interpretation of Dreams', Freud.

The following Louise Bourgeois images: 'The Family I,' 2007, Gouache on paper, suite of 12. 'Nothing to Remember' on hand-drawn music paper. 'Pregnant Woman', 2008. 'Pregnant Woman', 2007. 'Take me right back to the track', 1994. 'I do', 2010 archival dyes on cloth with embroidery. 'Maman', 1999.
Permission Art © The Easton Foundation/Licensed by VAGA, New York, NY

First Lacan http://en.wikipedia.org/wiki/Foreclosure (psychoanalysis) #cite_note-11.
Second Lacan http://en.wikipedia.org/wiki/Foreclosure (psychoanalysis) #cite_note-11.

'Reading Lacan', Jane Gallup 129ff.

O certainly, the pity of it, the pity and goats and monkeys..., 'Othello', Shakespeare.

All the definitions of words, except 'therapist', come from the online O.E.D.

'Was it a vision or a waking dream? Fled is that music: - Do I wake or sleep?' from the beautiful 'Ode to a Nightingale' by John Keats.

'All I have to Do is Dream.' The Everley Brothers. Del Bryant. Permission.

The newspaper cutting (p71) is from The Guardian 12 May 2013. Lucy Johnstone is a UK clinical psychologist, trainer, speaker and writer and a long-standing critic of biomedical model psychiatry. Lucy has authored a number of articles and chapters on topics such as psychiatric diagnosis, psychological effects of ECT, and the role of trauma in breakdown.

The front cover is a photograph of a detail from 'Song of the Hebrus' by Lynne Gibson. Permission. The photo is by A.A. Permission.

All other attributions are cited on the relevant pages.

---------------------------ARTS COUNCIL---------------------------

My thanks and appreciation to:

Steve White at 'One Digital' for embarking on this project and agreeing to buy a scanner! And Livvi White at 'OW-CH' for hours of highly skilled commitment and for being so easy to work with.

My many good friends for their friendship, some of whom were such encouraging readers along the way. I hope they know how very much it has meant to me to be able to share this story with them.

Annabel and Matthew, Imogen, Bryony, Saskia and Hugo. Miranda and Stewart, Sam and Callum; Theo and Kerry, Angela and Ailish for all their amazing support and love in so many ways. My sister, Jacky, especially for confirming things remembered. My brother, Michael, for stepping in immediately with love, financial assistance and affirmation of me. Kim, without whose support, love and consistent timely encouragement and very careful first-reads this book may never have existed.

My therapist with more than words can say for 'bearing' me so creatively, generously and positively throughout our work together.

My beloved P.A. for his support of all kinds, his love and his unfailing belief in the symbolic life.

The Arts Council: the production of this book was supported using public funding by Arts Council England.

LOTTERY FUNDED | ARTS COUNCIL ENGLAND — Supported using public funding by

one DIGITAL

OW-CH

www.ingramcontent.com/pod-product-compliance
Lightning Source LLC
Chambersburg PA
CBHW061011030426
42335CB00029B/3371

9 781956 864625